PM Story
TEACHERS'

Turquoise Level

He walked along in the middle of a forest of grey legs.

ANNETTE SMITH

NELSON PRICE MILBURN

Contents

About the PM Library

Story Books, Traditional Tales and Plays, and Animal Facts

The basic philosophy

'Children learn best with books that have meaning and are rewarding' ... *Reading in Junior Classes*, New Zealand Department of Education.

'I can read this!' All books in the PM Library are **centred on meaning**, but they are also designed to give children the rewarding experience of **success**. If a child can read one book they should be able to read another and another. Success should follow success. When the right match of 'child to book' is made, the greater the child's interest and the greater his or her desire to read.

On every page in every book care is taken with the sentence structures, the choice of words, the clear well-spaced type, and with the meaningful, accurate illustrations. Because the books are easy as well as interesting, children are able to practise a variety of reading skills and enjoy the feedback of success. They learn new words — and practise them again and again — all the time understanding what they are reading about, and returning to the books with pleasure *because* they have real meaning, and emotional impact.

The criticism levelled at many 'stories' written for beginners is that most are not stories — they are highly repetitive reading exercises in which meaning comes a poor second. Teachers and children have often been disappointed by the bland banality of most early school 'readers', with pages that were shaped not by a storyteller but by a need to repeat known words, or sentence structures or letter clusters, as often as possible. In revulsion from these interest-starved, over-repetitive non-literary exercises, some modern teachers have built their reading programs around library picture books that are worth reading for their own sake — only to discover that too many children are defeated when presented with 200 or so basic words in quick succession. It is not easy for average beginners to sort out *were was with will well would who why what when where which went want won't walk watch wall wait work wash warm word* ... it never will be!

The authors of the PM Library have worked hard to combine the virtues of two approaches — **controlled basic vocabulary** to let children master a growing number of common but confusing **high frequency** words, and **storytelling** quality to engage the mind and emotions and make learning to read satisfying. The authors have been well supported by a team of highly talented illustrators.

Features of the PM Story Books

The books have many ingredients, and all stories are rigorously considered and shaped to meet high standards.

All stories have:

- *meaningful content*. The situations and concepts can be understood by young children. The resolution in each story is logical — these stories encourage children to think by *letting* them think. The books are full of opportunities for intelligent discussion and logical prediction.
- *well-shaped plots*. Tension appears early in each story — something goes amiss — and the problem is solved by the end. It is tension that keeps children and teachers interested in the story — what will happen next? When the problem is finally resolved the ending is satisfying.
- *no sexism, racism or stereotyping of people*. Some women have supportive roles but others work — there is a female police officer and a female engineer. Jack's dad is a caregiver. Black, Asian and Caucasian children all have a turn at being central characters. The books include a boy with Down syndrome and a girl who uses a wheelchair, and the elderly, too, are shown leading active lives.
- *a wide spread of subjects* to meet the different experiences and enthusiasms of as many children as possible. There are stories about everyday life at home in the suburbs and at school; some stories are set in the inner city and others in the great outdoors. Toby, the tow truck who advises his driver, introduces readers to technology; this is fantasy that lifts children's understanding of the modern world.
  Another subset takes children back to the days of the dinosaurs; other stories look at modern animals (from elephants and beavers to guinea pigs and goldfish). Common natural crises — hailstorms, thunder, lightning and the pitch black night — provide drama and should help children face their fears, just as the characters in the stories do.
- *warmth and emotional sensitivity*. The child heroes are successful problem solvers — they are never laughed at, and never made to look inadequate. Animals are treated with sensitivity, too.
- *language that is satisfying to the ear*. The rhythms of good English — storyteller's English — are there. These stories pass the test of good literature and they sound satisfying when they are read aloud. The power of these stories is enhanced by balanced phrasing, and the right word in the right place.

- **considerable scientific accuracy**. Because accuracy matters, the dinosaur stories are carefully written to reflect recent research, and Toby the tow truck solves his towing problems in technically accurate ways. **All** stories are checked for accuracy.
- **well-designed typography**. At this level a serifed type face gives words coherance and individuality. The spacing of words, lines and paragraphs enhances readability. 'Plantin' is a classic typeface selected for its exceptional readability.
- **elisions**. These continue to be introduced at a steady rate: the 'n't' family now comes in.
- **a rate of new word introduction strictly held to 1 in 20**. When each new word is supported by at least 19 known words the decoding process is easier. Children are reading well away from frustration level. They are at a success level where reading is enjoyed. They are reading for pleasure and meaning. By the end of Orange Level children will have mastered about 350 high frequency (heavy duty) words as well as many interest words. It is reassuring to know that these 350 words account for about 75% of the words used in most passages of narrative English.
- **many opportunities to learn about the way words work**. At this stage of their reading children have to be able to turn written letters into spoken sounds, continue the sounds and check the message. The reading process depends on all three skills. When faced by a new word children need to be shown how to break it into syllables or letter clusters. Successful decoders have to be flexible and have enough confidence to keep trying. Confidence is built from past successes, from application of syntactic and semantic cues, and from mastery of words and letter clusters met before. Through experience, children will become aware that the vowel **a** is likely to represent one of five sounds: *a* as in *at*, or *ah*, or *ape* or *all*, or *ago*. In English it is flexibility that leads to successful decoding.
- **attractive well-drawn illustrations** that enable children to gain maximum understanding as they match picture with text, and vice versa. Meticulous care has been taken with these hardworking pictures. These are books that children will return to again and again with delight.

Features of the PM Traditional Tales and Plays

- **Although these stories are simplified short versions of the well-known tales, a great deal of the original flavour has been kept.** Most of the tales have been firmly anchored in time and place so that *The Three Billy Goats Gruff* is clearly Norwegian, *Stone Soup* reflects the poverty of the time in which it was written and *The Elves and the Shoemaker* belongs to the 17th century.

- **Each part in each play** is colour coded to lessen confusion and help children understand the conventions of a printed play.

Features of PM Animal Facts

- **Vocabulary is linked to the grading of the Story Books and Traditional Tales and Plays**. The grading logo, a coloured petal, indicates the recommended level for Guided Reading. As with the Story Books and Traditional Tales and Plays, the introduction of each new word is supported by 19 known words.
- **Non-fiction has a different 'dialect'**. Many sentences are short, and the necessary introduction of new interest words (mostly nouns) is accompanied by exact picture clues. Children reading non-fiction have to learn to link photographs and text and 'read' them together, as both inform. Each paragraph stands alone. Children do not have to hold the thread of a story in their minds as they read — pages can sometimes be read out of order, and the book approached through its index. All these things (short sentences, abundance of picture clues, absence of a developing plot) mean that many children find non-fiction less demanding than fiction, and even more enjoyable.
- **Non-fiction has a standard layout**, with new components that can be explored in PM Animal Facts, e.g. contents page, clear headings, labelled diagrams, alphabetical index.
- **A linear self-correcting program.** The questions at the foot of the page are not designed to make children research other books, nor to 'trick' them. Their purpose is to build confidence and to secure information. The immediate re-reading of a page of text to find or check an answer leads to careful thought, and greater retention of knowledge.
- **PM non-fiction books have reliable information**. Thorough research and scientific accuracy matter in all books in the PM Library, not least in the non-fiction books.
- **High interest levels**. In spite of their simplicity, these books arouse interest, e.g. Did you know that … birds evolved from dinosaurs? … bison are a type of cattle? … ponies are not baby horses? … goldfish can be black? … guinea pigs are called cavies? … some cats like vegetables? Even adults will learn something new.
- **Independent research**. The simplicity of the text and the clarity of the layout allows young children to taste the delights of independent discovery.
- **Links with the PM Story Books** increase children's understanding, adding depth to both strands. Many PM Story Books are supported by non-fiction titles: *Nelson the Baby Elephant* is matched with *Elephants* (PM Animal Facts: Animals in the Wild); *Two Little Goldfish* is matched with *Goldfish* (PM Animal Facts: Pets).

Using this Teachers' Guide

Before beginning the PM Story Books at Turquoise Level, children will have read the PM Story Books at the Red, Yellow, Blue, Green and Orange levels. They will have acquired at least 350 high frequency words and many other interest words. These books will have allowed the children to develop confidence, skills and independence, and to think critically about language and meaning. Predictability and logic are an essential part of these stories. It is this strong focus on logic and sense that helps children form the habit of self-correction. **Meaning** is the most important element in all PM Story Books.

The Teachers' Guides have been designed to assist busy teachers to plan and develop challenging language opportunities in their classrooms. The PM Story Books should be used with a wide variety of other books and materials to ensure that children succeed at each level before they proceed to the next. The ideas described in each Teachers' Guide can be adapted for other books.

There are Teachers' Guides for each colour level.

The large daisy logo has eight coloured petals showing the more advanced levels that follow the 12 of the daisy 'clock'. The eight are: Orange 1, Orange 2; Turquoise 3, Turquoise 4; Purple 5, Purple 6; Gold 7, Gold 8.

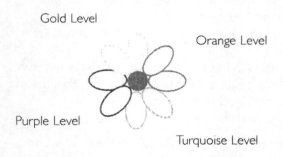

Gold Level

Orange Level

Purple Level

Turquoise Level

By the end of Gold Level children should have reading ages of 8+ years.

Teachers' Guides have also been compiled for the PM Traditional Tales and Plays, and Animals Facts books. Each Teachers' Guide has suggestions and ideas for guidance in the use of the PM books at that level.

Emphasis has been placed upon the development of the language skills — speaking, listening, reading, writing, viewing and presenting. These skills are common to all curriculum areas. Reading is not treated as a subject that stands alone.

Teacher information

This section contains notes about story content; shows the recommended reading level for each story; gives the number of running words used; and includes background information to support the teacher.

Creating the atmosphere

This is the 'tuning in' stage. It is the time when the teacher focuses the children's thinking on the content or concepts of the story. At this stage, related language or exciting new vocabulary can be discussed, written on the white board or sometimes acted out. In this way new ideas become familiar and the children's language is enriched.

Focusing on the story

Guided reading

Book study is an in-depth study of the story. It is a time to follow the plot, to become emotionally involved in the tension, the climax and above all to enjoy — perhaps predict — the satisfying ending.

It should be such an enjoyable experience that the children will want to read the book right through to the end all by themselves. Because new high frequency words have been introduced slowly and carefully in the books children can achieve this success.

Going beyond the story

Teachers may select from or adapt these language enrichment activities to suit the needs of their own classes. Some activities are suitable for small groups of children to work at together, others are for individuals.

Some may even be taken with a whole class. All have been designed to develop purposeful stimulating language. They give children ample opportunity to interact verbally not only with teachers but also with one another. Some activities in science and mathematics have been included to extend children's thinking and experiences beyond the story content. The art and drama activities will allow children opportunities to express themselves and help them to make sense of their reading.

Books to share and compare

These are suggested titles of books by other authors and from other publishers. Children need to have many stories read to them, often. They soon know that reading is enjoyable and will want to return to favourite books to read themselves. Occasional questions about the stories will sharpen the focus, prompt interest and talk, and ensure that children listen with understanding.

Reading aloud to children is one of the best ways of enriching their vocabulary and increasing their general knowledge.

Developing specific skills

It is important that these skills should be taught, but within the meaningful context of the child's current reading. They are not intended for teaching in isolation. As children gain an understanding of 'how words work' they will become confident to apply this knowledge to unfamiliar words.

Blackline masters

Blackline masters designed to challenge children's thinking are included with all Teachers' Guides. Each activity is for the individual child and can be completed independently and with a sense of success.

The children are encouraged to use their PM Story Books:
- to follow instructions, e.g. *Grandad's Mask*, *The Race to Green End*;
- to research the text, e.g. *The Cabin in the Hills*, *Rescuing Nelson*;
- to use and present visual information, e.g. *Jonathan Buys a Present*, *Bird's Eye View*;
- to extend vocabulary, e.g. *The Hailstorm*, *Little Dinosaur Escapes*;
- to apply personal experiences, e.g. *Monkey Tricks*, *Nelson, the Baby Elephant*;
- to apply understanding about words, e.g. *Toby and the Accident*, *Number Plates*.

For some Blackline masters at this level, checklists have been included to encourage the children to take more responsibility for their own learning.

Before the children begin work on the Blackline masters discuss the sheet with them to ensure they know what they are doing, why they are doing it and how they are to do it.

The Blackline masters in the Teachers' Guides have real purpose, engaging children in independent activities that increase their skills with language.

Language monitoring checks

Regular monitoring of children's progress is an essential part of sound teaching practice. Monitoring checks have been placed at the bottom of each page to guide teachers' observations of children's behaviours. They are the language skills, understandings and behaviours of speaking, listening, reading, writing, viewing and presenting that should be developing at that particular stage of language acquisition, e.g. Orange, Turquoise, Purple or Gold Levels. They are not specific to a particular book. Sometimes language monitoring checks can be used more formally as a checklist. (See page 24.)

The PM Story Books, with their rich language structures and strong storylines, provide excellent material for monitoring children's control over meaning, language structures and visual cues.

Running words

Having the number of running words available is useful when analysing the information from the reading record sheets.

Running words for these revised reading books follow these rules:
- The cover title and title page are not counted.
- Compound words are counted as one word.
- Hyphenated words, e.g. water-weed, are counted as one word.
- Animal and vehicle noises that include a vowel, e.g. Moo-oo, Toot-toot are one word.
- Sounds such as 'sh-sh-sh' and 'Mmm-Mmm' are not words.
- Numbers in numeral form, e.g. 1, 2, 3 are not words but when they are spelled out, e.g. one, two, three they are counted as a word.
- 'Mr' and 'Mrs' are counted as words.

Reading record sheets of the text of three books, one at each stage — Turquoise 3, Turquoise 3/4, Turquoise 4 — have been included on pages 26–28.

Procedures for administering and analysing running records can be found in Marie M. Clay's *An Observation Survey of Early Literacy Achievement* (Chapter 4, 'Taking Running Records of Reading Texts', Heinemann, Auckland, 1993).

The books at Turquoise Level

Running words 262

- When volcanoes erupt they can devastate the landscape. This is the story of an eruption that changed the lives of a group of dinosaurs. The long necked Apatosaurus lived in the Jurassic period.

Blackline master 1, p.31.

Running words 332

- Monkey behaviour and the care of animals kept in captivity are woven into this story about a monkey that escapes from the new cage at the zoo.

Blackline master 2, p.32.

When the Volcano Erupted

Creating the atmosphere

Make use of the information on the inside cover of the book. Let the children discuss what they know about volcanoes. Explain the words *erupt* and *lava*.

Focusing on the story — guided reading

- pp.2–3 — Ensure that children understand what is meant by 'the volcano stayed asleep'.
- pp.4–5 — Read these pages and discuss the vivid words — *shake, roared, rumbled, shot, flew, red-hot*.
- pp.6–7 — Ensure the children understand the concept of a *liquid* river of red-hot rock. Link the lava in the illustration with the printed word.
- pp.8–9 — Discuss the importance of escaping from an eruption.
- pp.10–13 — Scientists have found footprints on the bottoms of lakes made by Apatosaurus (or similar species) in just the same way as described here on these pages. The sauropods had their front legs touching the lake bottom and used their back legs occasionally to kick off when they changed direction.
- pp.14–16 — Ask the children to name the things that the dinosaurs really needed to keep themselves alive.

Monkey Tricks

Creating the atmosphere

Have the children share their knowledge and understanding of monkey behaviour from first hand observation at a zoo or from wildlife television programmes.

Focusing on the story — guided reading

- Read the title and study the cover illustration. Identify the two characters Rebecca and her friend, Amy, from the PM Story Book Orange Level *Rebecca and the Concert*. Predict some possible situations that could explain why Amy is pointing to the monkey.
- pp.2–3 — Notice that, although she is confined to a wheelchair, Amy is very independent. Amy's father refers to 'the new monkey house'. Discuss how and why most zoos are upgrading the living conditions for their animals. Ensure that on p.3 the children are aware that Rebecca and Amy are at a viewing window at the monkey house. Discuss the sign on the wall.
- pp.4–7 — The agility and intelligence of the monkey becomes evident. Talk about possible ways to capture it.
- pp.8–11 — Check that the children understand the reason why the zoo keepers brought the bananas and carried a net. Can the children guess who the zoo keeper in the white coat is and why she chose to stay by the tree?
- pp.12–15 — Explain some of the reasons why vets use dart guns to tranquilize animals. Ask the children to re-read the last paragraph on p.14. Reassure them that the monkey has just been sedated in order to capture it and to prevent injury.
- p.16 — The children may want to discuss how the zoo keepers will secure the monkey cage to prevent further escapes.

PM Story Books Teachers' Guide Turquoise Level (Set A)

The Cabin in the Hills

Creating the atmosphere

Read a story to the children about sleeping out in cabins or tents, e.g. *The Big Alfie Out of Doors Story Book* (Shirley Hughes, Bodley Head, 1992). Talk about the eerie sounds of some nocturnal wildlife, e.g. the hoot of an owl or the snuffle of a hedgehog.

Focusing on the story — guided reading

- Read the title. Study the cover and title page illustrations. Ensure that the children understand that the cabin is a place for basic shelter. The furnishings inside are usually very sparse, e.g. wooden bunks and benches, a wood burner stove for cooking and heating.
- pp.2–3 — Talk about the fact that brothers and sisters often squabble. Mitch, the younger brother, is asserting himself.
- pp.4–7 — Show the children how to read some of the text in a voice that reflects the tension of the storyline. Predict what might be in the cabin. Did anyone notice the end of the tail on p.5?
- pp.8–9 — Using the information from the text, ask the children to predict how they will get rid of the possum.
- pp.10–11 — Ask the children: what other noises could they have made to scare the possum?
- p.16 — Ask why Mitch was so sure that the cabin door had to be closed.

Developing specific skills

The following skills should be taught within the context of the children's reading of *When the Volcano Erupted*, *Monkey Tricks* and *The Cabin in the Hills*.

- **Revise blends and digraphs in the initial, medial and final positions**
  bl cl dr sm st str sw ch sh
- **Look at letter clusters**
  -ack -ast -et -ot
- **Discuss beginnings**
  a- e.g. *a*go, *a*gain   be- e.g. *be*came, *be*gan
- **Look at endings**
  -o e.g. ag*o*, volcan*o*   -er e.g. keep*er*, flow*er*
- **Talk about past tenses**

fly, flew	try, tried
come, came	hold, held
shine, shone	swim, swam
hide, hid	buy, bought
run, ran	keep, kept

- **Discuss adverbs**
  suddenly, carefully, safely, slowly, loudly
- **Clap the syllables**
  care/ful/ly, slow/ly, vol/can/o, e/rup/ted

Can the children express their understanding clearly and succinctly?
Can the children predict and make comparisons?

Running words   350

- Mitch and his family enjoy exploring the outdoors together. In this story they are going to spend the night in a cabin up in the hills but something unexpected happens.

Blackline master 3, p.33.

The brush tailed possum is a native of Australia and very common in New Zealand where it has been introduced.

Books to share and compare

- ***Volcanoes: Mountains that Blow their Tops,***
  Nicholas Nirgiotis,
  Grosset and Dunlap Inc., 1996.
- ***Make your own Paper Dinosaurs,***
  Sally and Stewart Walton,
  Salamander Books, 1994.
- ***Curious George Visits the Zoo,***
  Margret Rey and Alan J. Shalleck,
  Houghton Mifflin, 1989.
- ***Going to the Zoo,***
  Tom Paxton,
  Morrow, 1996.
- ***Sleep Out,***
  Carol Carrick,
  Houghton Mifflin and Clarion, 1973.
- ***Up North at the Cabin,***
  Marsha Wilson Chall,
  Lothrop, 1992.

Running words   359

• This new story about Jonathan and his parents is set in an inner city market. Jonathan tries to find just the right present for his grandfather. Jonathan Little has been met before in *Lost at the Fun Park*, *Pete Little* and *The Flying Fish*.

Blackline master 4, p.34.

Jonathan Buys a Present

Creating the atmosphere

Ask the children to share their experiences of shopping at a market. Introduce the word *stall*. Talk about the wide range of things that can be bought at a market. Discuss the noise and exciting atmosphere.

Focusing on the story — guided reading

• Read the title together and study the cover illustration. Re-introduce Jonathan as a character who has appeared in three other PM Story Books.
• pp.2–3 — Take time to study the market scene on these pages. Notice the different stalls, the stall holders and the cultures that make up the crowd. Ask the children to read these two pages and suggest why the book was given its title.
• pp.4–5 — Ask the children if there could have been another reason why Jonathan wanted to buy the toffee apple for Grandad.
• p.6 — After reading this page, ask the children to predict what Jonathan will do next.
• pp.8–9 — Discuss why Jonathan has now decided to keep the marbles rather than give them to Grandad. Ask the children why Jonathan has changed his mind.
• p.12 — Talk about Jonathan's anxiety and the new problem that he faces.
• pp.14–15 — After reading these pages, the children may want to guess what Jonathan has bought. Check how accurately the children use the text and illustrations to direct their predictions.
• p.16 — The children should be aware that both Mum and Dad are just as enthusiastic about Jonathan's choice of gift as he is himself.

Running words   348

• Cynthia Moss, a scientist, has lived beside herds of African elephants for many years. It is her meticulous research that inspired much of this story.

Blackline master 5, p.35.

Nelson, the Baby Elephant

Creating the atmosphere

Read PM Animal Facts: Animals in the Wild Turquoise Level *Elephants*, pp.4–6, to the children.

Focusing on the story — guided reading

• Look at the cover picture. Discuss the phrase: 'Baby elephants move in a forest of grey legs.'
• pp.2–5 — Before the children read the text, explain that elephants' trunks are like long noses. The adult elephants are smelling the new baby and are stroking him.
• pp.6–11 — Ask the children how old they were when they first started to walk. The focus of the story is now on Nelson's determination to walk in his first day of life. Being able to walk is a survival skill.
• pp.12–13 — Refer to PM Animal Facts: Animals in the Wild Turquoise Level *Elephants*. Page 5 of this book describes exactly how the calf drinks. Compare this photograph to the illustration in the story book.
• pp.14–16 — Enjoy the remainder of the story.

PM Story Books Teachers' Guide Turquoise Level (Set A)

Toby and the Accident

Creating the atmosphere

Re-read the three previous stories about Toby and BJ (PM Story Books Orange Level). List the situations that occurred in these stories. Talk about the way that Toby and BJ worked together to solve their problems.

Focusing on the story — guided reading

- Using the cover illustration, discuss what causes accidents.
- pp.2–3 — Observe the children's responses to these two opening pages. Many children will enjoy noticing similarities in all four books. Do the children understand why BJ checked the flashing lights on Toby's cab?
- pp.4–7 — Explore the text and find the problems that Toby and BJ now have ahead of them. Look carefully at the illustrations. Discuss how the people from the power company have used ladders and a strong brace to secure the pole.
- p.9 — Explain why Toby had to keep his brakes on hard. (It is the car that should move not the tow truck.)
- pp.10–11 — Discuss this additional problem.
- pp.12–13 — The intrepid Toby and BJ work together, as always, and pull the car safely away from the pole.
- p.16 — Read this final page together with appropriate intonation.

Running words   324

- BJ and his animated towtruck, Toby, are now old friends from the PM Story Books. Once again Toby and BJ have been called out by the police. This time they have to help at a traffic accident.

Blackline master 6, p.36.

Developing specific skills

The following skills should be taught within the context of the children's reading of *Jonathan Buys a Present, Nelson, the Baby Elephant* and *Toby and the Accident*.

- **Revise blends and digraphs in the initial, medial and final positions**
    cl fl pl cr br fr gr dr str tr sm st ch sh
- **Look at letter clusters**
    -all -ould -ight -own -ack
- **Talk about past tenses**

buy, bought	give, gave	fall, fell
come, came	stand, stood	

- **Discuss adverbs**
    slowly, wobbly
- **Look at comparatives**
    fast, faster   strong, stronger   slow, slower
- **Suggest opposites for**

start	_____	over	_____
slower	_____	big	_____
push	_____	old	_____

- **Revise contractions**
    I'll, I'm, I've   here's, that's   can't, don't, isn't

Additional language features to discuss
- <u>a</u> present but <u>an</u> accident
- *wind*
    "I'll keep my brakes on hard while the rope *winds* in," said Toby.
    The *wind* blew the leaves off the tree.

Books to share and compare

- *A Present for Paul*,
  Bernard Ashley,
  HarperCollins, 1996.
- *Bouncing Buffalo*,
  Posy Simmonds,
  Cape, 1994.
  (Red Fox edition 1996.)
- *Jumbo*
  Rhonda Blumberg,
  Bradbury, 1992.
- *Little Elephant Thunderfoot*,
  Sally Grindley,
  Orchard, 1996.
- *How Many Trucks Can a Tow Truck Tow?*,
  Charlotte Pomerantz,
  Random House, 1987.

Can the children read silently without interruption?
Do the children understand many words in context?

Running words 395

- Little Dinosaur (who always has to escape from Big Dinosaur) has his most terrifying adventure yet. Although this story is fiction, Little Dinosaur is modelled on Comsognathus and Big Dinosaur on Megalasaurus. Both belong to the Jurassic period, before the evolution of flowering plants.

Blackline master 7, p.37.

Little Dinosaur Escapes

Creating the atmosphere

Re-read *A Lucky Day for Little Dinosaur* and *The Dinosaur Chase*.

Focusing on the story — guided reading

- Ask the children to define the word 'escapes'. What do they think Little Dinosaur is escaping from?
- pp.2–5 — Have the children read these pages to themselves. Discuss the concept of a *dry* river bed.
- pp.6–11 — Talk about clouds, lightning, thunder and rain and how they are connected.
- p.12 — Talk about the power of a flash flood.
- p.16 — Little Dinosaur escapes from three things. What were they? Re-read the story to find out.
- At a further reading identify how one event causes the next. Ask the children some 'why' questions, e.g. Why did the log roll? Why was Little Dinosaur trapped? Why did the dry river bed fill with water?
- Cause and effect shapes this story.

Rescuing Nelson

Running words 367

- *Rescuing Nelson* is the second story about Nelson the baby elephant. It describes a possible event in the life of a baby elephant.

Blackline master 8, p.38.

Creating the atmosphere

Read pp.7–9 of PM Animal Facts: Animals in the Wild Turquoise Level *Elephants* and discuss the importance of water and mud to wild African elephants.

Focusing on the story — guided reading

- Read the title and talk about the word 'rescuing'. Ask the children what they think could be going wrong.
- pp.2–3 — The text should help children to understand that Nelson is still very young.
- pp.4–7 — The information on these pages is reinforced in PM Animal Facts: Animals in the wild Turquoise Level *Elephants*.
- pp.8–9 — Make sure that children realise that Nelson is in serious danger.
- pp.10–13 — Pause at these illustrations. Study them carefully. Ensure that the children know that the herd is concerned about Nelson.
- pp.14–15 — After the children have read these pages ask them what Nelson's grandmother did to help him.
- p.16 — Enjoy the satisfactory ending. Notice Nelson's body language.

PM Story Books Teachers' Guide Turquoise Level (Set B)

Number Plates

Creating the atmosphere

All children want to be accepted as normal people who can get on with their lives. Read and discuss the story *Don't Forget Tom*.

Focusing on the story — guided reading

- Focus on the title and talk about number plates. Do the children know the number plate of their family's car?
- pp.2–3 — Have the children read this page and discuss William's age and the activities he could do at school. Notice the books on William's desk.
- pp.4–5 — After reading these pages ask the children to predict which number plate William and Charlotte will find next.
- pp.8–9 — Make sure everyone has spotted William in the family car.
- pp.10–13 — Read on and discuss the events that have happened on these pages. Can any of the children predict what will happen next?
- pp.14–16 — Discuss why William's presence of mind gave the whole family special pleasure.

Running words   412

- William has Down's syndrome, a genetic condition. There is a wide range of ability among children with Down's syndrome. Some of them can cope in mainstream classrooms and acquire many skills.

Blackline master 9, p.39.

Developing specific skills

The following skills should be taught within the context of the children's reading of *Little Dinosaur Escapes, Rescuing Nelson* and *Number Plates*.

- **Revise blends and digraphs in the initial, medial and final positions**
  bl cl fl pl sl br cr dr fr
  sc sk st sw ch ph sh th
- **Look at endings**
  -er   river, water, thunder, number, letter, swimmer, driver, teacher, hotter, clever
- **Talk about past tenses**
  sitting, sat   find, found   swim, swam
  spring, sprang   lie, lay
- **Discuss compound words**
  sometimes, outside, supermarket, anyone, without
- **Clap the syllables**
  res/cu/ing, grand/moth/er, e/nor/mous, su/per/mar/ket

Additional language features to discuss

- **Two adjectives strengthen the noun**
  deep dark mud   wise old grandmother
- **Prepositions influence the verb**

rolled over	rolled onto	rolled across
lit up	landed on	raced towards
roared down	pushed over	lay down
carried away	sitting on	

Books to share and compare

- *100 Questions and Answers: Dinosaurs and other Prehistoric Animals,* John Cooper, Puffin, 1993.
- *Daniel's Dinosaurs,* Mary Carmine, Scholastic, 1997.
- *Nelson, the Baby Elephant,* Beverley Randell, Nelson, 1997.
- *Don't Forget Tom,* Hanne Larsen, Adam and Charles Black, 1974.
- *He's My Brother,* Joe Lasker, Whitman, 1974.

Do the children study detail in print to assist their control over meaning?
Can the children follow simple directions from print?

Running words 511

- Traffic education is an important part of the school curriculum. Strong safety messages are reinforced in a memorable way in this story.

Blackline master 10, p.40.

Running words 396

- The fascination of large vehicles captures the imagination of many children. In this story, the main character, Luke, goes to the truck depot with his father one Saturday morning and helps to find a lost child.

Blackline master 11, p.41.

Reading is about broadening children's understanding of the world around them.

The Seat Belt Song

Creating the atmosphere

Discuss safe behaviour in cars. Possible points to raise include: wearing seat belts at all times, locking doors and using special car seats for babies.

Focusing on the story — guided reading

- Read the title and discuss the cover illustration. Talk about the characters. Ask the children to predict where this might be happening.
- pp.2–3 — Some observant children will identify Luke and Andrew from PM Story Books Orange Level *Roller Blades for Luke*. Note that both books have been written by Jenny Giles and illustrated by Rachel Tonkin.
- Identify the new character, Zoë, on the cover illustration.
- pp.4–5 — Read the words of 'The Seat Belt Song' with the children, then sing it together to the familiar tune of Twinkle Twinkle Little Star.
- p.6 — As the children read this page independently, ask them to find the important safety message.
- pp.8–9 — Ask the children why the word *click* has been written four times. Observe strategies used by the children as they decode the word *siren*.
- pp.10–11 — Discuss how the words *flashed* and *screamed* give stronger meaning to the text.
- pp.12–15 — Ensure that the children notice that Andrew is kind to Zoë, that Officer Young praises both Zoë and Andrew, and that Andrew talks about his mistake.
- p.16 — Talk about the reason for the italic type and indented text of the seat belt song on this page.

Bird's Eye View

Creating the atmosphere

Show the children photographs of large trucks which are used for long distance road haulage. Talk about the size of the vehicles, their length and height from the ground.

Focusing on the story — guided reading

- Study the cover illustration. Identify the character Luke from PM Story Books Orange Level *Roller Blades for Luke*.
- pp.2–3 — Look closely at the illustration. Discuss the busy scene and the word 'depot'. Compare the height of the truck drivers to the size of their vehicles.
- pp.4–5 — Notice how Luke's father has to climb up two very high steps to get into the cab of his truck. Luke's dad has to check the tyres. Encourage those children who are familiar with large trucks to share their knowledge about necessary maintenance.
- pp.6–7 — This page explains what is meant by *a bird's eye view*. Remind children about the title of the book.
- pp.8–9 — Encourage the children to put themselves in Luke's place as they study the scene from high up in the cab of the truck.
- pp.10–11 — Notice the urgency in the illustration and the text.
- pp.12–13 — Logic and reasoning are evident in Luke's response to the boy. This page builds on the information given on p.9.
- p.16 — The satisfactory conclusion to the story reinforces the meaning of the expression *a bird's eye view*.

The Hailstorm

Creating the atmosphere

Ask the children to describe hail. Write these statements on a chart. Refer to some dictionaries for additional definitions.

Focusing on the story — guided reading

- Study the cover illustration. Discuss where the girls might be and what they are doing. Some children will recognise the character Zoë from PM Story Books Turquoise Level *The Seat Belt Song*.
- pp.2–3 — Read the words that Miss Bell said to the children. Pattern the urgency of the situation. Ensure that the children are aware that rainstorms can happen very quickly.
- pp.4–7 — 'Read' the illustrations. Notice the distance from the sports equipment shed to the classroom.
- pp.8–9 — Zoë's fear will be felt as the children read the text and link the meaning with her actions and expression.
- pp.10–13 — The girls' problem has increased. Ask the children to locate the words that describe their situation and their fear, e.g. *louder, rattled, hit, bounced, darker, colder.*
- pp.14–15 — Ask the children to find the words that describe Zoë and Kylie's relief.
- p.16 — Much discussion could follow the reading of Zoë's last statement. Why did she say the hail was beautiful?

Developing specific skills

The following skills should be taught within the context of the children's reading of *The Seat Belt Song*, *Bird's Eye View* and *The Hailstorm*.

- **Revise blends and digraphs in the initial, medial and final positions**
  bl   cl   pl   sk   sm   st
- **Look at letter clusters that have the same sound**
  -ar—car, start, yard   -ou—out, ground, cloud
  -ong—song, along   -ick—trick, click
- **Look at letter clusters that do *not* have the same sound**
  se*a*t, h*ea*d   s*oo*n, g*oo*d, d*oo*r   d*ow*n, wind*ow*
- **Discuss beginnings**
  a-   e.g. about, along, across, away   be-   e.g. behind
- **Talk about past tenses**
  sing, sang   run, ran   fall, fell
  forget, forgot   give, gave   grow, grew
- **Discuss adverbs**
  tightly, carefully, slowly
- **Discuss new compound words**
  anywhere, classroom, hailstorm, doorway
- **Revise contractions**
  I'm, It's, I've, can't, couldn't, don't, isn't
- **Look at comparatives**
  loud, louder   dark, darker   cold, colder
- **Clap the syllables**
  po/lice/man, off/ic/ers, Sat/ur/day, e/ve/ry/thing

Do the children recognise the title, author and title page of a book?
Do the children display enjoyment in sharing reading experiences?

Running words   386

- In this story, two young girls have to cope with the frightening sounds of a hailstorm in a rather scary situation. The theme is 'overcoming fear'.

Blackline master 12, p.42.

Books to share and compare

- ***Look Out on the Road**,*
  Paul Humphrey and Alex Ramsay,
  Evans Brothers Ltd, 1994.
- ***Watch Out on the Road**,*
  Elizabeth Clark,
  Wayland, 1991.
- ***Mighty Machines: Truck**,*
  Claire Llewellyn,
  Puffin Books, 1995.
- ***Big Dan's Moving Van**,*
  Leslie McGuire,
  Random House, 1993.
- ***An Evening at Alfie's**,*
  Shirley Hughes,
  The Bodley Head, 1984.
  (Red Fox edition 1995.)
- ***Harry's Stormy Night**,*
  Una Leavy,
  Orchard Books, 1994.
- ***Jess Was the Brave One**,*
  Jean Little,
  Viking Puffin, 1991.

Grandad's Mask

Creating the atmosphere

Ask the children to re-read *Jonathan Buys a Present* (PM Story Books Turquoise Level). Notice pp.15 and 16. This story is its sequel.

Focusing on the story — guided reading

- Talk about the cover illustration. Discuss Jonathan's actions and Grandad's reaction.
- pp.2–3 — Discuss the video tele-intercom systems found in apartment blocks.
- pp.4–5 — Ask the children to find the dialogue that shows the warmth of Jonathan's relationship with his grandfather.
- pp.6–7 — Although a jammed lift could be a frightening experience, Grandad explains what to do.
- pp.8–9 — Before they read the text, encourage the children to 'read' the three illustrations in sequence. Grandad loves playing tricks. Ask the children to explain Grandad's actions to support this statement.
- pp.10–11 — Repairs to the lift would have to be carried out in the *Lift Machine Room* at the top of the building. Note the engineer's reassuring comment.
- pp.12–13 — Again, Grandad wears the mask to 'perform' his next trick.
- pp.14–15 — Do the children understand that Mum and Dad have run up the stairs to the fourth floor?
- p.16 — Discuss the engineer's joking comment.

Running words 441

- Jonathan and his parents visit Grandad who lives in an apartment building. This is another story that should encourage prediction and reasoning. 'Reading the pictures' helps the children to understand the story.

Blackline master 13, p.43.

Ant City

Creating the atmosphere

Talk about traffic in a busy city: the noise and the movement of the vehicles and the people.

Focusing on the story — guided reading

- Read the title, the names of the author and the illustrator to the children. Study the cover illustration together. Look closely at the details. Compare the size of the ants with the crumbs and the shoes. Ask the children why they think the story is called *Ant City*.
- pp.2–3 — Read p.2 to the children, patterning long pauses at the end of each paragraph to exaggerate the time lag reflected in Georgia's pensive expression.
- pp.4–5 — Check that children are integrating meaning, syntax and visual cues as they read.
- pp.6–7— Most children will relate to Georgia's emotions as she struggles to cope with Becky's remark.
- pp.8–13 — Georgia's curiosity will seem very natural to most children. They will enjoy her satisfaction as she shares her discovery with big brother Danny.
- p.14 — Allow time for the children to think about the text, to understand the link between the ants and the city traffic.
- p.16 — Talk about Georgia's change in attitude. Why is time no longer a problem? Georgia has taken the cheese from her school bag and is keen to continue looking at ant behaviour. Ask the children to talk about their own observations of ants.

Running words 393

- Time seems to pass slowly in situations when children have to wait for an adult. This is a story about a sensitive young girl and her emotions. Georgia lives in a large inner city apartment building in the USA.

Blackline master 14, p.44.

Georgia says 'Mom' because she lives in the USA. Can children spot other American things in the illustrations?

PM Story Books Teachers' Guide Turquoise Level (Set C)

The Nesting Place

Creating the atmosphere

Tell the children that Maiasaura means 'good mother reptile'. The dinosaur was given this name because she fed and cared for her babies in nests, in much the same way as birds do.

Focusing on the story — guided reading

- Read the title. Talk about the nest made of mud and lined with leaves.
- pp.2–3 — Before reading the text notice that there are nests as far as the eye can see. This is why the book is called *The Nesting Place*. Help the children to imagine the size of the adult Maiasaura (7 metres or 23 feet long). If necessary, explain the term 'on the move'.
- pp.4–7 — Discuss briefly the making of the nests and the laying of the eggs. Ask the children what made the eggs hatch if the mother didn't sit on them. Have the children read and find out why Long-head is leaving the hatchlings.
- pp.10–11 — The story tension increases with the appearance of the meat-eating dinosaur. Encourage the children to read on to find out what happens.
- pp.12–15 — Children may like to interrupt their reading and count the babies on pp.10–11 and now on p.14. This subplot is important to the story. Ask the children to suggest reasons why the mothers on the outside of the nesting place ended up with fewer hatchlings. (There is a parallel with penguin colonies today.)
- p.16 — Ask the children which Maiasaura is Long-head. Justify their answers. (The point of the story will have been made). Talk about the three dots (ellipses). They suggest time passing. This is a story that goes on and on and on.

Developing specific skills

The following skills should be taught within the context of the children's reading of *Grandad's Mask*, *Ant City* and *The Nesting Place*.

- **Revise blends and digraphs in the initial, medial and final positions**
  br cr fr gr pr str thr st ch sh
- **Use PM Alphabet Blends books for**
  soft c — city   soft g — Georgia
- **Suggest new words that rhyme with**
  soon, look, back, light, fast
- **Look at endings**
  -er e.g. corner, cracker
  -y e.g. busy, noisy, city
- **Talk about silent letters**
  *k*now   crum*b*
- **Look at verb tenses**
  fix, fixes, fixing, fixed
  throw, throws, throwing, threw
- **Discuss plurals**
  bus, buses   baby, babies   leaf, leaves

Can the children read their own writing for meaning and spelling accuracy?
Can the children use simple word sources to correct their spelling?

Running words   356

- This is another book about the days of the dinosaurs, based closely on the latest scientific research. A Maiasaura nesting site was discovered in 1978 in North America. Dozens of nests had been built just the length of one adult Maiasaura apart. In the nests were half-grown hatchlings who must have been fed by their parents for many weeks.

Blackline master 15, p.45.

Books to share and compare

- **Grandfather and I,** Helen Buckley, Lothrop, 1994.
- **Matthew and Tilly,** Rebecca C Jones, Dutton, 1991.
- **Amazing Grace,** Mary Hoffman, Frances Lincoln, 1991.
- **Basil, the Loneliest Boy in the Block,** Jason Timlock, Puffin, 1990.
- **Dinosaur Lives,** Priscilla Hannaford, Ladybird, 1997. (See pp.22–3 for Maiasaura.)
- **Dinosaurs, an A–Z Guide,** Michael Benton, Kingfisher, 1988.

Jordan's Lucky Day

Running words   463

- This is a narrative with fast moving tension. Jordan, a new character to the PM Story Books, and his friends, meet a football star in an unexpected way.

Blackline master 16, p.46.

A *hat trick* in football means scoring three goals.

Creating the atmosphere

Have the children talk about the different physical activities that they play outdoors with their friends. Ask them to give reasons why some of the places that these games are played are safer than other places.

Focusing on the story — guided reading

- Read the title, the author's name and the illustrator's name to the children.
- pp.2–3 — Study the illustration. Talk about the boys' actions and the involvement of everyone in their game. Help the children to identify the main characters: Jordan, in the pink shirt, and Kris, in the yellow shirt. Discuss why Kris called to Jordan, 'It must be your lucky day'.
- pp.4–5 — After the children have read p.4 discuss the use of the word *darted*.
- pp.6–7 — Discuss the reaction of the characters and link the illustration with the text.
- pp.8–9 — Talk about Jordan's honesty and apology. Discuss the reactions of the man as he involves the boys in solving their problem.
- pp.10–11 — Discuss why Steve Parker's name was known to Jordan.
- pp.12–15 — Ask children who play football to suggest some of the skills that Steve Parker might have demonstrated.
- p.16 — Discuss the practice of football stars signing their autographs on T-shirts and footballs. The football will become a treasure for Jordan. It will help him remember the safety messages and the football skills that were taught to him by a football hero.

Riding to Craggy Rock

Running words   385

- *Riding to Craggy Rock* is a sequel to PM Story Books Turquoise Level *The Cabin in the Hills.* In this story, Mitch and Ben and their parents are mountain-biking in the hills when a thunderstorm strikes. The boys learn the safe way to behave in a thunderstorm.

Blackline master 19, p.47.

Creating the atmosphere

Have the children re-read *Mitch to the Rescue* and *The Cabin in the Hills*. Discuss the characters and their love of the outdoors.

Focusing on the story — guided reading

- Discuss the cover illustration. Notice the oval design used in all three books. Establish where the characters are standing and what they are doing.
- pp.2–3 — Talk about some features of mountain bikes that make them different from road bikes, e.g. handlebars, frame design, gears, tyres. Draw conclusions about why these differences are necessary. Ask the children to suggest a reason for Mum's remark on p.3. Notice other safety precautions taken by the family, e.g. helmets, sturdy footwear, long trousers.
- pp.4–9 — Direct the children to read the end of this section. Discuss the situation with them before they read on.
- pp.10–13 — Discuss thunder and lightning and torrential rain. Make sure that all the children know what is the safe thing to do in a thunderstorm.
- pp.14–16 — Ensure that children understand Mitch's observations and remarks about the tree that has been struck by lightning.

PM Story Books Teachers' Guide Turquoise Level (Set C)

The Race to Green End

Creating the atmosphere

Group the children into pairs. Give them a die, a shaker and two counters. Turn to pp.8–9 of the storybook and have them play the game — The Race to Green End.

Focusing on the story — guided reading

- As the children read the story, have additional books available, open at the board game, for children to play as the story unfolds. To get the most value from the book have the children read it in pairs.
- The rules for starting are set out very clearly. Make sure children understand the rule about throwing a six to start.
- Play the board game according to the events in the story.
- Ask the children who they think is going to win and why.
- Ask a child who has a bike to explain what happens when they ride it on loose stones.
- At the completion of the reading discuss the moral of the story.

Running words   508

- Children are highly motivated to read instructions printed on interesting board games.

Blackline master 18, p.48.

There are 155 words to read in the instructions on pp.8–9.

Developing specific skills

The following skills should be taught within the context of the children's reading of *Jordan's Lucky Day*, *Riding to Craggy Rock* and *The Race to Green End*.

- **Revise blends and digraphs in the initial, medial and final positions**
  br cr dr fr gr tr thr wr sk sm st ch sh
- **Look at letter clusters that have the same sound**

-ar	e.g. farm	-all	e.g. small
-et	e.g. wet	-ot	e.g. got
-ill	e.g. still	-ay	e.g. way
-ut	e.g. but	-ast	e.g. last
-ow	e.g. throw	-iny	e.g. shiny

- **Discuss beginnings**
  a-   across, around, another, along
- **Look at endings**
  -er   corner, footballer, shiver, under, better, newer, blacker
  -y   shiny, sorry, lucky
- **Talk about silent letters**
  *k*new, *w*rote
- **Discuss past tenses**

ride, rode	throw, threw
win, won	try, tried

- **Discuss compound words**
  football, driveway, something, somewhere, himself, motorbike, goodbye, mudguard, inside, upside
- **Revise contractions**
  I'm, I'll, It's, I've   can't, didn't, don't, wasn't   there's, that's

Additional language features to discuss
- to, too, two   there, their   threw, through
- **Descriptive verbs can follow a noun to increase its strength**
  Thunder rumbled and growled.

Books to share and compare

- ***Willie the Wizard***, Anthony Browne, Julia McCrae, 1995.
- ***Pass it, Polly***, Sarah Garland, The Bodley Head, 1994.
- ***The Hare and the Tortoise***, Retold by Jenny Giles, Nelson, 1998.
- ***The Hare and the Tortoise***, Retold by Carol Jones, Angus and Robertson, 1996.
- ***The Magical Bicycle***, Berlie Doherty, HarperCollins, 1995.

Can the children sustain their own writing for longer periods?
Can the children give their opinion on live perfomances and videos?

Going beyond the story

- Ask the children to re-read **When the Volcano Erupted** paying particular attention to the volcanic activity. Look closely at the illustration on pp.6–7. Discuss the details including the red-hot lava, the trees, the fire and the black smoke.

  As a group activity the children could make a papier mâché model of the volcano. Using information from this story book and from other sources, e.g. television documentaries, help the children to write a short explanation of a volcanic eruption.

- Study a newspaper item of local interest to the children. Talk about the heading and features of the language used. Explain a simple framework for writing this type of text. Have the children write a newspaper report of the incident at the zoo in the story book **Monkey Tricks**. The children could draw the 'photograph' that they think would be likely to accompany the report.

- Have a group of children retell the story **The Cabin in the Hills** as an enlarged comic strip for the wall. Encourage them to work co-operatively as they make decisions about the selection of text to be used and about the illustrations.

- Ask the children to rewrite the story **Jonathan Buys a Present** using the same storyline but this time include different items that Jonathan could have chosen for his grandfather. Give a reason for the selection of each new item. Include a surprise on the last page.

- Using the dialogue from the book **Toby and the Accident**, the children could role play the story. They will have to make decisions about important characters including Toby. As a shared group activity help the children write the story in play format. Refer to the plays in PM Traditional Tales and Plays (Orange and Turquoise levels).

- With the children, search the text of **Little Dinosaur Escapes** to find action words that give strong visual images. Ask the children to suggest other words that convey a similar action, e.g.

Little Dinosaur	sprang		The log	wobbled
	jumped			shook
	leapt			moved
	stepped			rolled

Finish writing each sentence using the new words in turn. Discuss how some words describe an action more vividly than others.

Choose language and form to present information.

Understand the purpose of a different text form.

Experiment with an alternative way of presenting text.

Justify choice of alternatives.

Contribute to discussions respecting the views of others.

Experiment with alternatives to express similar meaning.

- Sing **The Seat Belt Song**. Read the words of the song carefully with the children. Identify the lines of text that convey the important safety messages, e.g. 'Find the seat belt', 'Pull it down'. Talk about other situations where safety is very important, e.g. walking through carparks, crossing roads. Choose a situation, e.g. the car park. Discuss rhyming words related to this theme, e.g. walk/talk, car/far. As a guided writing activity innovate the words of *The Seat Belt Song* to suit.

Respond to familiar text and construct a new meaning.

- Have children role play a television interview based on the rescue of the little girl in the story book **A Bird's Eye View**. Choose an announcer who will describe the situation, e.g. 'Early this morning, a little girl … '. Follow this announcement with the interview. The children can make decisions about the characters from the story, e.g. who should be interviewed and what questions will the reporter ask? After the role play write the questions and answers on a chart. Encourage the children to assess the appropriateness of the questions and answers. Give reasons.

Communicate ideas using drama.

- **Grandad's Mask** is a sequel to **Jonathan Buys a Present** (PM Story Books Turquoise Level). Identify and list the series of events in both books, e.g.

Think critically and discuss selected parts of a text.

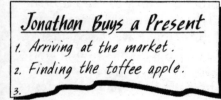

Use these lists to retell the stories in more detail, e.g.

 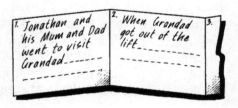

- Use the word 'hailstorm' to explore new words related to weather.

Explore language to extend personal vocabulary.

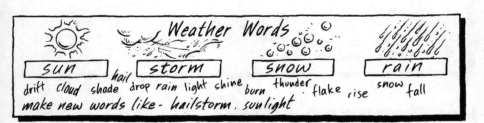

When the children have made their lists they should discuss them with a friend and use a simple dictionary to check the accuracy of the words. They could write some words in sentences to emphasise the meaning.

- Re-read the story **Riding to Craggy Rock**. On a chart, list descriptive words or phrases that can be found on each page, e.g.

As a group, discuss how these words draw the reader emotionally into the story.

- Discuss the signs on the supermaket window and in the car park on pp.8–9 of **Number Plates**. Talk about other signs that are likely to be found in the supermarket and at the car park. Explain that visual signs, including number plates, convey a message. Emphasise the importance of the shape of the sign, the layout and the use of colour. As a paired activity the children could design and write the signs that they may see
  — at a supermarket,
  — at a zoo (refer pp.2–3 *Monkey Tricks*), or
  — at a building site (refer *Toby and the Big Red Van*).

- Jordan and his friends meet a football hero in **Jordan's Lucky Day**. The children could talk about local sports heroes. Invite one of these people to the classroom. This will involve much planning. Have the children write a letter or design a personal invitation. Discuss the wording and layout of both text forms. Prepare questions. Write the questions on card for some children to practise prior to the visit. Reinforce courtesies when listening and speaking. Teach the children how to make 'thankyou' speeches and how to write 'thankyou' letters.

- Re-read *The cross-country race* (PM Story Books Green Level) and **The Race to Green End**. Play the board game on pp.8–9 following the written instructions. Discuss how written instructions guide the players. As a paired activity make up a maths game about a cross country race or an obstacle course. Write instruction cards for when a counter lands on a green coloured space 'Good luck' and for when a counter lands on a red coloured space 'Bad luck'.

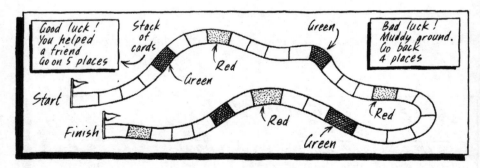

Ideas for science

Re-read **Ant City** and *Mrs Spider's beautiful web* (PM Story Books Green Level). Using the information from the texts and illustrations of both books, list facts about ants and spiders on a grid.

From this information write comparison statements, e.g. 'Ants have six legs', 'Spiders have…'

	Body features	Body features	Body features
Ants			
Spiders			

- Re-read **The Nesting Place** and *Pterosaur's Long Flight* (PM Story Books Orange Level). Both books are set in the cretacious period. Use these two books and *The Clever Penguins* (PM Story Books Green Level), as well as additional material from the library, to compare how the Maiasaura and Pterosaurs both fed and cared for their babies in much the same way as birds do today. Present the information in project form.

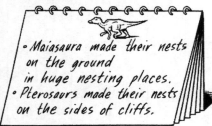

- Re-read **Nelson, the Baby Elephant** and **Rescuing Nelson**. Search both the texts and the illustrations for information about elephant behaviour. Have the children record these facts on a large wall chart and illustrate appropriately.

- Some children could extend this activity by collating the facts recorded on the above chart. Write this information into individual booklets and include a contents page.

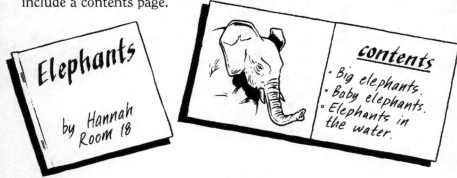

- Read PM Animal Facts: Animals in the Wild *Elephants*. Compare the information found in the story books and the non-fiction book.

Language monitoring checks

Speaking / Listening		Reading / Writing		Viewing / Presenting				
Turquoise Level *Skills, understandings and behaviours*	Miles	Phoebe	Stephen	Georgia				
• Express understanding clearly and succinctly	✔	✔	✔	✔				*3/11*
• Can predict and make comparisons	✔	✔	✗	✗				*4/11*
• Can read silently without interruption								
• Understands many words in context								
• Studies detail in print to assist control over meaning								
• Can follow simple directions from print								
• Recognises title, author and title page								
• Displays enjoyment in sharing reading experiences								
• Reads own writing for meaning and spelling accuracy								
• Can use simple word sources to correct spelling								
• Can sustain own writing for longer periods								
• Gives opinions on live performances and videos								

General comments *(Date all observations)*

Language monitoring checks

	Speaking / Listening		Reading / Writing		Viewing / Presenting			

Turquoise Level
Skills, understandings and behaviours

• Express understanding clearly and succinctly								
• Can predict and make comparisons								
• Can read silently without interruption								
• Understands many words in context								
• Studies detail in print to assist control over meaning								
• Can follow simple directions from print								
• Recognises title, author and title page								
• Displays enjoyment in sharing reading experiences								
• Reads own writing for meaning and spelling accuracy								
• Can use simple word sources to correct spelling								
• Can sustain own writing for longer periods								
• Gives opinions on live performances and videos								

General comments (Date all observations)

Reading record

Name: Age: Date:

Text: *Nelson, the Baby Elephant*   Turquoise 3 R.W. 123

Summary

Page		E	S.C.	Errors MSV	Self Corrections MSV
2.	When Nelson, the new baby elephant, was born, all the other elephants in his family came to look at him.				
3.	His wise old grandmother was there first. His aunts came, his cousins came, and his big sister came.				
4.	All the elephants in Nelson's family stood around watching him. They made happy noises. They waved their trunks about because they were so pleased that he had been born.				
5.	At first, Nelson lay on the ground. He did not look at his wise old grandmother, or his aunts, or his cousins, or his big sister. He was too new.				
6.	But soon he was very busy trying to stand up. Nelson had four new wobbly legs and it was hard for him to make them work.				

Reading record

Name: _____   Age: _____   Date: _____

Text: *The Hailstorm*   Turquoise 3/4   R.W. 126

Summary _____

_____

Page		E	S.C.	Errors MSV	Self Corrections MSV
3.	Zoë looked up at the sky as she ran to catch a ball.				
	"Miss Bell!" she called. "Look at those big black clouds!				
	They are coming right over us."				
	"Yes, they are," said Miss Bell. "It's going to rain.				
	Back to the classroom, everyone!				
	Zoë and Kylie, will you please put away the box of balls?"				
4.	Zoë and Kylie hurried to the shed with the balls.				
	But Zoë dropped her end of the box.				
	Some of the balls fell out and bounced down the steps.				
	The girls chased after them.				
	"Hurry up!" laughed Kylie. "It's starting to rain."				
6.	Zoë picked up the last ball, and ran to the shed with it.				
9.	"Oh, look!" said Kylie.				
	"We can't get back to the classroom. It's raining too hard."				

Reading record

Name: Age: Date:

Text: *Riding to Craggy Rock*   Turquoise 4 R.W. 122

Summary

Page		E	S.C.	Errors MSV	Self Corrections MSV
2.	One morning, Mitch and Ben and Mum and Dad set off from the cabin on their bikes. "Craggy Rock is my favourite place for a picnic," said Mitch. "I can't wait to get there."				
3.	"It's going to be a long ride," said Ben. "Yes," said Mum, "just as well we have our water bottles with us. We will need to drink a lot of water on a warm day like today."				
4.	The sun was hot, and the air was very still. "We can stop for a drink at the top of the next big hill," said Dad. "There's a good look-out up there."				
5.	The boys led the way. At last, they came to the look-out at the top of the big hill.				

Reading record

Name: Age: Date:

Text: Turquoise   R.W.

Summary

Page		E	S.C.	Errors MSV	Self Corrections MSV

Using the Blackline masters

Before using each Blackline master prepare the children as follows:

Blackline master 1 *When the Volcano Erupted*
- Reinforce the importance of saying and hearing sounds within words.
- Encourage the children to use context as they attempt to write each word.
- Use other Turquoise Level Set A Story Books and PM Alphabet Blends to help when writing more words beginning with sm–, st–, fl–.

Blackline master 2 *Monkey Tricks*
- Help the children to organise their ideas by using the key words. Give examples, e.g. 'One Saturday morning . . .', 'One Saturday before lunch . . .', 'One Saturday in the holidays . . .'.

Blackline master 3 *The Cabin in the Hills*
- Re-read the story book and discuss the text associated with each illustration identified on the Blackline master.
- Ask the children to write their own text for each illustration.

Blackline master 4 *Jonathan Buys a Present*
- Study the illustration on pp. 2–3. Talk about all the items for sale, e.g. bags, belts, oranges.
- Revise the procedure for ordering words alphabetically.

Blackline master 5 *Nelson, the Baby Elephant*
- Study the cover illustration of *Rescuing Nelson*. Notice that the baby elephant is crying with fear and frustration.
- Guide the children in their reading of both books to search for other examples of behaviour that is similar to that of human behaviour.

Blackline master 6 *Toby and the Accident*
- Emphasise the importance of looking carefully at details in print.
- Scan across the words 'cheered' and 'checked'. Notice similarities and differences.
- Talk about the –ly ending that helps us to understand how an action takes place.

Blackline master 7 *Little Dinosaur Escapes*
- Discuss the vivid action words in the example— 'wobbled' and 'rolled'.
- Have the children suggest sentences, e.g. I wobbled down the path on my skateboard.

Blackline master 8 *Rescuing Nelson*
- Talk about how a story is made up of a problem, increasing tension leading to a climax. This will help the children understand the four sections of the Blackline master to be completed in their own words.

Blackline master 9 *Number Plates*
- Discuss the spelling guidelines in section 1 of the Blackline master.

- The quality of the children's sentence writing is an indication of those who need additional assistance.

Blackline master 10 *The Seat Belt Song*
- Before the children begin the Blackline master, discuss the many visitors who come into the classroom to assist them with their learning, e.g. the principal, the school nurse, the reading teacher, parents, older children etc.

Blackline master 11 *Bird's Eye View*
- Emphasise that organisation of visual language involves much thought and planning.
- Ensure the children understand the written instructions.
- Encourage peer discussion and evaluation.

Blackline master 12 *The Hailstorm*
- Ensure the children understand the three parts to this Blackline master—compound words, comparatives and descriptive words (adjectives). (The answers for sections 2 and 3 will not be found precisely in the story book.)

Blackline master 13 *Grandad's Mask*
- Have the children read the instructions and explain them to a friend.
- Encourage them to be creative.
- A strip of card at the back of the mask will help to secure it when it is worn.

Blackline master 14 *Ant City*
- Talk about the content of this book review.
- Explain what is meant by main characters and minor characters.
- Ask the children to describe Georgia's personality from their own understanding of the storyline.
- Encourage personal response to the text.

Blackline master 15 *The Nesting Place*
- Discuss each section of the Blackline master. Ensure the children understand what is required before they proceed independently.

Blackline master 16 *Jordan's Lucky Day*
- Revise the procedure for completing a crossword. Suggest that the children now write the letters as capitals.

Blackline master 17 *Riding to Craggy Rock*
- Section 1. Take the children's thinking beyond the reasons given. Help them to understand the deeper meaning behind each statement.
- Section 3. Illustrating precisely each of the opposites will generate much discussion.

Blackline master 18 *The Race to Green End*
- Re-read the instructions on the board game of the story book pp. 8–9.
- Share ideas for themes, pictures and written instructions.

Name: _____ Date: _____

Fill in the missing words.

Say the words **slowly** as you write them.

Can you **hear** the first two letters of the words?

A long time ago some dinosaurs lived in a forest.

They had leaves to eat and water to _____.

The volcano _____ asleep and life was good.

But one day the volcano _____ to shake.

It roared and it rumbled.

Red-hot rocks _____ into the air.

The big _____ dinosaurs could not get out

of the way. Some of them were hit

by _____ rocks. The red-hot lava set fire

to the _____. Soon all the forest was on fire

and _____ smoke filled the air.

• Now check your spelling.

• You will find the words

  on pages 2–7

  of the story book.

Words I need to
learn how to spell.

  •

  •

Turn this page over and write three words

that begin with '**sm**', '**st**' and '**fl**'.

Name: _____ Date: _____

One Saturday Amy and Rebecca went to the zoo.

Write and draw about something **you** did one Saturday.

These words will help you plan your story:

| When? | Where? | Who? | Why? | What? |

Begin your story by answering the **when** question.

One Saturday _____

_____

_____

_____

_____

Name: _____ Date: _____

Look carefully at every picture in **Jonathan Buys a Present**.

Make a list of ten things sold at the market.

1   6

2   7

3   8

4   9

5   10

Use a dictionary to check your spelling.

Now write your list of words in **alphabetical** order.

1   6

2   7

3   8

4   9

5   10

Ask a friend to check your list.

Name: _____   Date: _____

Read **Nelson, the Baby Elephant** and **Rescuing Nelson**.

Draw and write three facts about elephant babies

that are similar to human babies.

Elephant babies	Human babies
1	
_____	_____
_____	_____
2	
_____	_____
_____	_____
3	
_____	_____
_____	_____

Name: _____ Date: _____

1. Write the correct word in each space.

BJ _____ the flashing light.

<table>
<tr><td>cheered</td></tr>
<tr><td>checked</td></tr>
</table>

The pole had a _____ .

<table>
<tr><td>crack</td></tr>
<tr><td>crash</td></tr>
</table>

"I'll keep my _____ on,"
said Toby.

<table>
<tr><td>bridge</td></tr>
<tr><td>brakes</td></tr>
</table>

The car _____ to move.

<table>
<tr><td>stopped</td></tr>
<tr><td>started</td></tr>
</table>

This time the pole _____ still.

<table>
<tr><td>stayed</td></tr>
<tr><td>started</td></tr>
</table>

BJ fixed the towing _____ under
the front of the car.

<table>
<tr><td>frame</td></tr>
<tr><td>fright</td></tr>
</table>

2. Make lists of words that rhyme.

down	back	light	flash
_own	_ack	_ight	_ash
_own	_ack	_ight	_ash

3. Toby pulled the car **carefully** away from the pole.

Write a sentence using each of these words.

slowly _____

_____

wobbly _____

_____

Name: _____ Date: _____

Little Dinosaur Escapes is a story
that is filled with exciting **action** words.

The log **wobbled** and then it **rolled** onto
Little Dinosaur's leg.

Wobbled and **rolled** are action words.
They help to make the story exciting.

Read the story again and make a list
of some more action words.

_____   _____

_____   _____

_____   _____

_____   _____

Now choose any three action words from the story
and write an exciting sentence using each one.

1. _____

_____

2. _____

_____

3. _____

_____

Turn this page over and draw a picture
about your most exciting sentence.

Name: _____   Date: _____

Retell the story **Rescuing Nelson**.
Read the pages then write the story
in your own words.

One very hot day,
Nelson the baby elephant
went down to a mud pool with his family.
They all put mud on their sides
and their backs and their heads.

Pages 8–11
Then _____

Pages 12–13
After that _____

_____

Pages 14–15
But _____

_____

Page 16
At last _____

_____

Rescuing Nelson © Nelson ITP, 1998.

1. Look in the story book **Number Plates**
and find the word to go in each space.

look	looking	looked
swim	_____	swam
stop	_____	stopped
race	_____	raced
go	_____	gone
find	finding	_____
make	making	_____

- **Say** each word.
- **Listen** to its sound.
- **Look** at the pattern of the word.
- **Say** the word again.

William _____ a long way down the pool.

The white car _____ out of the car park.

The driver _____ the wheels spin.

2. Write your own sentences with these words.

number _____

letter _____

driver _____

Number Plates © Nelson ITP, 1998.   Blackline master **9**   39

his page may be photocopied for educational use within the purchasing institution.

Name: _____ Date: _____

Officer Williams and Officer Young came to school
to talk about seat belts.
Make a list of four people
who come into your classroom.
Write about how they help you.

1. _____

_____

_____

2. _____

_____

_____

3. _____

_____

_____

4. _____

_____

_____

Name: _____ Date: _____

Luke had a **bird's eye view** from way up high in his father's truck.

Pretend that you are way up high in an aeroplane and you have a bird's eye view of your school and your playground.

Here are some of the things you might see.

- The classrooms
- The office
- The library
- The playground

List some more things you might see.

- _____
- _____
- _____
- _____

Turn this page over and draw a bird's eye view plan of your school.

When you have finished, check each thing on the list.
Make sure you have drawn it on your plan.

Show your plan to a friend.

Name: _____ Date: _____

1. **Hailstorm** is a compound word because
   it is made up of **hail** and **storm**.
   Look in the story book *The Hailstorm*
   and find four more compound words.

   _____   _____

   _____   _____

2. **loud**   **louder**

   The noise of the rain was loud
   but the sound of the hail was louder.

   dark   **darker**

   _____

   _____

   cold   **colder**

   _____

   _____

3. **Old** and **wet** are words that describe ropes.

   Describe these words. | old, wet ropes |

   _____ , _____ clouds   _____ , _____ hail

   _____ , _____ balls   _____ , _____ doors

Jonathan surprised his Grandad with the mask.

Make a mask to surprise someone in your family.

- Cut out the mask shape.
- Glue it onto thin card.
- Cut out the new mask.
- Decorate the mask.

You will need:
- card
- scissors
- paint
- stapler
- glue
- decorations

Name: _____ Date: _____

Title: ***Ant City***

Author: _____

Illustrator: _____

The main character _____

_____

The story was about _____

_____

_____

_____

_____

I think that _____

_____

_____

When I read this story,
I learned that ants

_____

_____   **an ant**

Name: _____ Date: _____

1. [st] Look for these letters in **The Nesting Place**.
          Sometimes they are at the beginning,
          the middle or at the end of words.

st _____ , st _____ , ____ st ____ ,

_____st, _____st, _____st.

2. **Plural** means more than one.

1 egg, 5 eggs	1 tree, 5 trees

The spelling of each of these plural words is tricky.

1 baby, 5_____	1 leaf, 5_____

Look in your story book to check your spelling.

3. [lucky]   [hurry]   [many]   [empty]   [ready]

There were a great _____ nests.

Now that her nest was _____ Long-head could lay her eggs.

Long-head had to _____ away to get food for her babies.

Long-head was _____ . She had eight babies left.

The enormous nesting place would be _____ again, until next year.

e Nesting Place © Nelson ITP, 1998.

his page may be photocopied for educational use within the purchasing institution.

Name: _____ Date: _____

Across

1. Jordan kicked the _____ .

3. The man _____ up the ball.

5. The gate will stop it
   from going onto the _____ .

7. Jordan said, "I _____ you."

8. The man _____ them
   how to pass the ball.

10. Steve took a pen
    from his _____ .

Down

2. The ball _____ out
   onto the road.

4. The ball bounced away _____
   the driveway.

6. They put a gate _____
   the driveway.

9. After a while, Steve looked
   at his _____ .
   "I'll have to go," he said.

1. Why did Mum say, "We will need to drink a lot of water on a warm day like today?"

_____

_____

Why did Day say, "We'll have to go back to the cabin. We are all too wet to get to Craggy Rock today."

_____

_____

2. We'll   means   **we**   **will**

   That's   means   _____   _____

   I'm   means   _____   _____

   Let's   means   _____   _____

   can't   means   _____   _____

3. Write opposites for

   stop   _____   warm _____

   first   _____   long _____

   coming _____   dark _____

Turn this page over and draw pictures to show these sets of opposite words.

     up, down   under, over

     in, out   on, off

This is a board game for you to make.

Choose a title for your game.

Draw the little pictures.

Write names for special places.

Write instructions in each bubble space.

Now play the game with a friend.

The Race to _____

ST____

Good luck!

1 2 3 4 5

6 7 8 9 10

Bad luck!

Bad luck!

11 12 13 14 15 16

Good luck!

17 18 19 20